THE WHALE

Giant of the Oce

Valérie Tracqui

Photos by L'Agence PHO.N.E.

French series editor, Valérie Tracqui

Charlesbridge

© 2004 by Charlesbridge Publishing. Translated by Randi Rivers.

© 2003 by Editions Milan under the title *La Baleine*
300 rue Léon-Joulin, 31101 Toulouse Cedex 100, France
French series editor, Valérie Tracqui

Published by Charlesbridge
85 Main Street
Watertown, MA 02472
(617) 926-0329
www.charlesbridge.com

Library of Congress Cataloging-in-Publication Data
Tracqui, Valérie.
  [Baleine. English]
  The whale, giant of the ocean / Valérie Tracqui ;
[translated by Randi Rivers].
    p. cm.
Summary: Presents the anatomy, behavior, life cycle, and
endangered status of the humpback whale, and briefly
introduces other whale species.
  ISBN 1-57091-625-X (softcover)
  1. Humpback whale—Juvenile literature. 2. Whales—Juvenile
literature. [1. Humpback whale. 2. Whales. 3. Endangered
species.] I. Title.
  QL737.C424T72813   2004
  599.5'25—dc22   2003011475

Printed in China
(sc) 10 9 8 7 6 5 4 3 2 1

PHOTO CREDITS
PHO.N.E Agency:
F. Gohier: cover and back cover, 1, 4–5, 5 (top), 6 (top), 7 (top), 8 (top and
bottom), 10–11, 10 (bottom right and left), 11 (bottom), 16 (bottom), 17 (top),
24 (bottom), 26 (top and bottom), 27 (top, middle, and bottom); R. Walter:
5 (bottom), 7 (bottom), 13 (bottom), 15 (bottom), 16 (top), 20 (bottom),
25 (bottom); J.-P. Ferrero: 12–13; M. Osmond: 22–23

A. Rosenfeld: 6 (bottom), 9, 14, 15 (top), 18–19, 19, 20 (top), 21, 24–25
M. Carwardine/BIOS: 17 (bottom)

"THAR SHE BLOWS!"

Summer is a magical season in Alaska. Over a period of many weeks, the sun warms the earth and the sea. During this thaw, glaciers break up and icebergs melt. Life blooms and food is abundant. Animals come out to feed. Drifting on sea ice, a polar bear catches the scent of seals, while marine birds circle overhead looking for a school of fish.

Suddenly a white plume bursts from the ocean. It sounds like a cannon blast. The noise is a humpback whale taking a breath. The white plume, or spout, can reach almost 10 feet high. The whale quickly inhales, then closes its blowholes. Two white flippers rise out of the water, and then the whale arches its back and sends its tail high in the air before disappearing. It has dived into the depths.

Humpback whales are recognizable by their 2 flippers, which measure a third of their total body length. Their name comes from the hump that appears in front of their dorsal fin when they bend their body to dive.

When whales exhale, a smell of rotten fish and rancid oil fills the air. The spout is a mixture of air, water vapor, and mucus. Spout formations vary with the whale species.

Each lobe of a whale's tail is called a "fluke." Tail size varies from species to species. A humpback's tail can measure 18 feet wide.

VERY SENSITIVE

Whales have sensitive skin, especially on their head and tail. Their sense of smell, however, is weak. As whales reach adulthood the organs that detect smell shrink, and scientists are therefore unsure how well adult whales can smell. On the other hand, whales have excellent hearing, even though their ears are only tiny openings on each side of their head.

Humpbacks have one hair on each of the small bumps on their face. Scientists believe these hairs may be able to detect obstacles in the same way cats' whiskers do.

Due to the lack of light underwater, whales' eyes are adapted for low-light conditions. Whales do not have tear ducts, but their eyelids secrete an oily substance that moistens and cleans their eyes.

When whales leap out of the water into the air, it is called "breaching."

Whales have good eyesight. On the dark ocean bottom, whales can open their pupils to let in light; then they can reduce their pupils in brighter areas. Although humpbacks are not the largest whales, they measure 45 to 50 feet long and weigh 25 to 40 tons. A thick layer of blubber helps whales survive in the cold water. Once out of the water, however, whales are soon too hot. To cool their body, whales increase the circulation to their flippers, dorsal fin, and tail.

Giants of the Ocean

There are three suborders of whales: Mysticeti (baleen whales), Odontoceti (toothed whales), and Archaeoceti (now extinct). Baleen whales, such as humpbacks and blue whales, are the largest animals on the planet. All whales are warm-blooded mammals, not fish. They need to return to the  water's surface to breathe air. Scientists believe that modern whales are descended from ancient land mammals. To live in the water, their bodies lengthened, their arms became fins, and their legs disappeared. Whales' tails are made of connective tissue and are not the remains of legs, as seals' tails are.

ADAPTED TO THE OCEAN

Whales use their flippers to steer and to slow down. A humpback's flippers are gigantic and white. Flipper size and color vary by species. Propelled by the movements of their tail, whales are fast and powerful swimmers. Before diving, whales renew about 80 to 90 percent of the air in their lungs, while humans replace only 20 percent when breathing.

Baleen whales close their 2 blowholes with a muscular flap when diving.

A humpback whale's flippers can measure up to 4 feet wide and 16 feet long.

Whales do not dive to great depths, but their bodies are adapted to conserve oxygen and energy when they do dive. Their heartbeat slows down. More oxygen is supplied to the heart, lungs, and brain, while other organs receive less. Whales can reach a depth of 80 feet without effort, and they can stay underwater for up to 20 minutes. Humpback whales can dive to 485 feet. When they need air, whales return to the surface.

The whale's reproductive organs are hidden inside its body to keep the whale's body streamlined.

THE FEAST

During the summer at the North Pole, plankton blooms and drifts on currents. Plankton is made up of tiny plants and animals, such as krill, that whales eat. Different whales have various ways of collecting food. Opening their large mouth, humpback whales take in 1,500 gallons of water. Their throat grooves expand, allowing more water to fill their mouth. When humpbacks close their mouth, their throat grooves contract, forcing water out the sides of their mouth. Baleen keeps in plankton, shrimp, and small fish.

To cover their energy needs, whales take in 80 to 130 mouthfuls of plankton-filled water each day.

Baleen

Baleen is strips of keratin, the same material as our fingernails. Baleen is fixed to a whale's upper jaw, lined up like bristles of a broom. The color and length of baleen vary according to the whale species. Baleen of the gray whale is about two to 10 inches long, while the humpback's baleen reaches about 30 inches. Colors range from black to white to yellow.

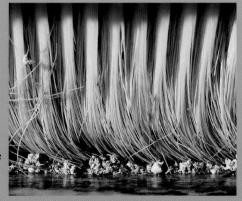

During the summer, whales eat enough food each day to equal 5 percent of their body weight. Their menu: plankton, shrimp, mollusks, herring, sardines, and anchovies. In winter, whales hardly eat at all.

Unfolding its 20 throat grooves like an accordion, a humpback whale can enormously increase the volume of its mouth.

Sometimes humpbacks hunt in groups using a method called bubble net feeding. A whale dives underwater, then spirals up to the surface while blowing bubbles through its blowholes. Thousands of bubbles form a net that traps the plankton on the surface. The whales then shoot up one by one, opening their huge mouths to take in the plankton.

MIGRATION

In September the water at the North Pole starts to freeze. Whales leave the Arctic, traveling in small groups called pods, to begin their migration. How do they find their way to the equator? It is a mystery. Some people believe that whales get their bearings by watching the sky, the coast, and the ocean floor, as well as by sensing changes in water temperature and magnetic fields.

Whales cover about seven miles per hour and travel between 1,800 and 4,000 miles, depending on the species. Humpback whales from Alaska take three months to migrate south and arrive near the equator in December. Humpback whales that feed in Antarctica take one and a half months to reach the equator. But the two humpback whale populations never meet—their journeys are separated by six months—because winter and summer are reversed in the two hemispheres. Once they arrive in warmer waters, humpback whales gather in small groups and search for a mate.

Humpback whales migrate for about a third of their life. They come to tropical zones from the Arctic or Antarctica. But all whales' routes remain a mystery because no one has been able to follow them in the immense ocean.

In this position, with its head straight out of the water, the whale is said to be "spyhopping."

LOVE SONGS

A strange song rises up through the ocean: a kind of powerful lowing that changes into a murmur. The male humpback whale tilts his head down and sings for 15 minutes without taking a breath. Females listen as this extraordinary song travels through the water for miles. Soon other males answer, varying the notes and their order. Researchers think the songs may communicate to females that males are ready to mate. The songs may also be a male's way of letting other males know that he is willing to compete for a female.

All whales use body language to communicate excitement or anger. They may slap their flippers or tail on the water. Some males even use spouts to indicate anger or aggression toward competing males. However they do it, their goal is the same: to attract a female.

Male whales sing, but scientists believe that females don't sing.

To attract attention the male swings a flipper in the air and rolls on his back. Then he taps his flippers on the water, one after the other, like he is beating a drum.

The male lifts his tail in the air and slams it on the water, making a noise that sounds like thunder. Then he waits for a female to answer.

Whale Song Research

Although all whales make sounds, only a few species' sounds are considered songs. Using hydrophones, scientists record humpback whales' mysterious melodies. With this technology, scientists hope to identify pods that return each year after migrating. The only question remaining is how to interpret the songs. Each song uses different moans, grunts, cries, and whistles. This makes the task of interpretation even more difficult.

FINDING A MATE

It is time to mate, and a small pod of whales looks for a sheltered bay. The group is made up of several males and a mature female. The dominant male from the pod escorts the female. Another whale challenges the dominant one. The challenger is insistent, brushing against the female and blocking her path. The female will swim away if she is not interested.

If the female is not ready to mate, she will swim or roll away.

To appear bigger, the male humpback fills its throat with air.

It takes incredible force to propel a whale's weight into the air.

The dominant male blows a bubble net to block the challenger's vision. This prevents the challenger from seeing the dominant male's flipper until it is too late. The dominant male slaps the challenger, then rushes him in a fit of anger. Like a torpedo, the challenger breaches, then falls on his side in a spray of foam. The challenger leaves. It is useless to fight a larger whale. The victor receives the female's attention, and they will mate.

Some fights are terrible; males receive cuts to the tail and the head.

A GIANT BABY

The following winter, females
return to the warm waters where
their babies were conceived to
give birth. In the shelter of a
shallow bay, mother whales bring
their babies, called calves, into
the world, tail first. Whales
usually have only one calf; twins
are rare. Newborn humpback
whales measure about 13 feet
and weigh close to a ton, but
they are clumsy. A mother
pushes her calf to the surface so
it can take its first breath. Then
the hungry calf begins to nurse.
Calves nurse underwater but stay
close to the surface so they can
get air. They drink 130 gallons
of milk each day and double
their birth weight in two weeks
(it takes six months for human
babies to do this). Calves nurse
for about four months to a year.

All year a calf follows its mother
like a shadow. The bond
between a mother and her calf is
strong. A calf learns its mother's
gestures, sounds, and travel
routes. A mother teaches her calf
where to find food and where
dangers lurk.

While a calf nurses,
its mother fasts and
loses a lot of weight.

A mother feeds her calf just under the surface of the water so that they can each breathe from time to time.

SCHOOLTIME

At first a calf stays close to its mother. It swims in its mother's wake, or path, without effort. The calf is pulled along by the current, or slipstream, its mother produces. Their bodies move in unison. The calf is playful and climbs on its mother's back and drums on her face. The mother nuzzles her calf. She would give her life for it.

At the end of several months, calves get bolder. Calves do not hesitate to leave their mother to play and spin. But calves are careful not to wander too far away.

Calves are not independent until they reach the age of 2 years.

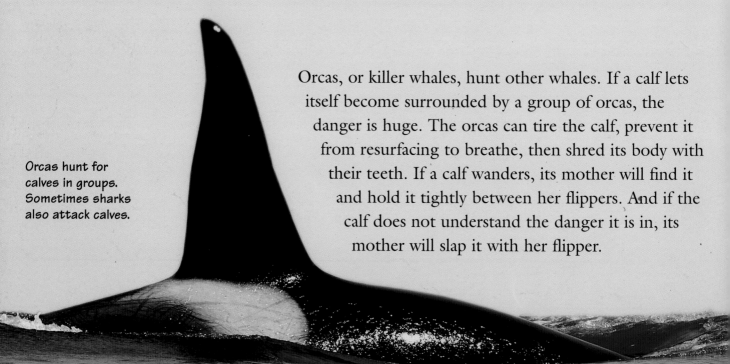

Orcas hunt for calves in groups. Sometimes sharks also attack calves.

Orcas, or killer whales, hunt other whales. If a calf lets itself become surrounded by a group of orcas, the danger is huge. The orcas can tire the calf, prevent it from resurfacing to breathe, then shred its body with their teeth. If a calf wanders, its mother will find it and hold it tightly between her flippers. And if the calf does not understand the danger it is in, its mother will slap it with her flipper.

A mother occupies herself solely with her calf. If it becomes an orphan, the calf will not be placed in the care of other females.

NEW JOURNEY

All during the winter, whales stay near the equator. The adult females are thin because they have had next to nothing to eat. They wait until their young are strong enough to make the journey back to their feeding grounds. Soon the moment arrives. Worried and nervous, whales slam their flippers and tails. Calves stick close to their mother. Soon an older female sets off on her route followed by several others. They will return next season after feeding on the generous supply of Arctic plankton—ready to fill the ocean with mysterious songs.

If they avoid hunters, pollution, and predators, whales can live from 30 to 100 years, depending on the species.

All these animals have a language of body movements that is unique to them. Perhaps one day we will understand them.

WHAT FUTURE?

Massacred for their flesh and oil, whales risk extinction. Laws now protect these fantastic creatures, but they are still in danger. Some whales are poisoned by pollution; others fall victim to disease, predators, or accidents.

The Japanese, Koreans, and Norwegians continue to hunt whales in the name of research.

Swimming with whales is an unforgettable adventure, but they demand patience and respect. The presence of these mammals underwater is magical.

KILLED WITHOUT MERCY

The whale industry reached its peak by the 19th century. Floating factories processed whale blubber on site, and the entire whale was used. Today people have invented products that replace whale by-products, and the hunt is not justifiable. From 1904 to 1980 two million whales were killed, at a rate of 100 per day. Not surprisingly, after such carnage a number of whale species were on the verge of extinction. In 1780 there were 150,000 humpbacks. Today there are fewer than 20,000.

PEACE SANCTUARIES

The Southern Ocean Sanctuary, created in 1994, protects whale feeding grounds in Antarctica. In 1997 the Hawaiian Islands Humpback Whale National Marine Sanctuary was established to protect the North Pacific population of humpback whales. Then in 1999 the International Mediterranean Sea Cetacean Sanctuary opened. One thousand rorqual whales (blue, minke, and humpback) find refuge there each year. In these sanctuaries and in others around the world, there are laws in place to protect whales; hunting, capturing, or mutilating them is banned.

A FRAGILE PROTECTION

Aside from sanctuaries there are also organizations that seek to protect whales. The International Whaling Commission (IWC) was created in 1946 to regulate whaling around the world. Today the IWC tracks whale populations and suggests whale management proposals to its members. The Marine Mammal Protection Act (MMPA) made it illegal to hunt or harass marine mammals in the United States. The hope is that these measures will save whales from extinction.

Whale Watching

In Rurutu, an island in French Polynesia, protection laws also apply to approaching whales. People want to ensure that tourists do not bother whales. Boats are not allowed within 165 feet of a whale. This distance increases to 330 feet if a calf is accompanying the adult whale.

Exceptions are made for researchers. Scientists study individual whales, which can be identified by the form and coloration of their tail.

BALEEN WHALES

Humpback whales are part of a suborder called Mysticeti, or baleen whales. Families in this suborder include the Balaenopteridae, or rorquals, and the Balaenidae, or right whales. Rorqual whales, such as humpbacks, have long bodies, a dorsal fin, and throat grooves. Right whales have long baleen, but they don't have a dorsal fin or throat grooves. Eschrichtiidae (gray whales) and Neobalaenidae (pygmy right whales) make up the other two families in this suborder.

GRAY WHALE

The only living member of the Eschrichtiidae family, gray whales have gray skin and only two short throat grooves. Unlike other whales, gray whales suck up sediment filled with crustaceans and filter out what they don't eat through their baleen.

SOUTHERN RIGHT WHALE

Southern right whales are easy to recognize by the huge calluses around their blowholes, eyes, and mouth. Like humpbacks, right whales feed on krill. Southern right whales were hunted excessively for their silky baleen and abundant oil. Today there are fewer than 4,000 in existence.

Fin Whale

Fin whales, also called common rorquals, are dark or brownish gray on top and white underneath. They are identifiable by their triangular head. Fin whales strain krill through their baleen and eat it while swimming on their side. Known as the fastest of the large whales, fin whales can reach speeds of 35 miles per hour.

Blue Whale

Blue whales have the distinction of being the largest animals on the planet. These giant rorquals measure 75 to 80 feet long and weigh an average of 130 tons. Blue whales can eat up to four tons of krill each day.

FOR FURTHER READING ON WHALES . . .

Gunzi, Christiane. *The Best Book of Whales and Dolphins.* Boston, MA: Larousse Kingfisher Chambers, 2001.

Roop, Connie, and Peter Roop. *Whales and Dolphins* (Hello Reader!). New York, NY: Cartwheel Books, 2002.

Rosenthal, Sue. *Whales.* New York, NY: Scholastic, 2003.

USE THE INTERNET TO FIND OUT MORE ABOUT WHALES . . .

Baleen Whales

—This site is a Sea World Education Department resource. It is filled with information about the life cycle of various whale species and offers conservation information as well. The site includes photos and helpful illustrations.

http://www.seaworld.org/infobooks/Baleen/home.html

Humpback Whales ACS Fact Sheet

—For more information about humpback whales, including physical descriptions of them, check out the American Cetacean Society's Web site. This site also has a natural history of humpbacks.

http://www.acsonline.org/factpack/humpback.htm

PBS—The Voyage of *Odyssey*

—This is a wonderful site from PBS that tracks the ship *Odyssey* and its crew's mission to study the health of the world's oceans. Visitors can hear whale songs, view vivid color photos, and learn more about cetaceans and ocean life.

http://www.pbs.org/odyssey/

INDEX

Anatomy 4–5, 6–7, 8–9, 10
Baleen 10
Baleen whales 7, 8, 26–27
Blowhole 4, 8, 11
Calves 18–19, 20–21, 22
Communication 14–15
Diving .4, 8, 11
Feeding 10–11, 22
Fighting .16–17
Flippers 4, 8, 15, 17, 20
Food 10–11, 18

Leaping 7, 17
Learning 18, 20
Migration 12–13, 22
Predators 20, 22, 24
Protection 24–25
Reproduction 9, 17, 18
Respiration 4–5, 7, 8, 14, 20
Senses 6–7
Songs 14–15
Swimming 4, 8, 20
Whale hunting 24
Whale watching 25